THE
CALM
IN THE
CHAOS

DR. SHELIA MCGREW, ThD.

DEDICATION

I would like to dedicate this book in loving memory of my wonderful, loving, anointed mother, Minister Annie Bell McGrew. Also, I want to dedicate this project in remembrance of my dear, sweet brother, Tommie Lee McGrew. We all love and miss you all very much.

CONTENT

ACKNOWLEDGMENTS

First, I would like to Thank God for giving me grace, favor, insight, and guidance concerning His Word and promises for my life. I thank Him for His guidance in writing this book to inspire others as well as myself, as we navigate through turbulent times. To my very supportive father, Bishop Walter McGrew Sr., I say, "Thank You" for faithfully and consistently listening to my Sunday morning broadcasts, encouraging me in your own words to, "Hold On Daughter". To all of my support family, brother, sisters, nieces, nephews, in-laws, cousins, friends, radio listeners, Facebook watchers/ followers, etc. I appreciate you and pray that every moment of chaos be overpowered by God's unlimited calming grace and peace. Also, I wish to acknowledge and thank, my sister, Gloria McGrew Everett for helping me complete this project.

INTRODUCTION

Life is a precious gift from God. Living the life that God ordained for His people from the beginning of time to its fullest can be obtained. The exciting and incredible aspect of life is the limitless opportunities and satisfaction of achieving goals. It is easy to be happy and positive when everything is well, but what should we do when life challenges are not so favorable? As 2019 was coming to an end, and 2020 was on the horizon, I was inspired to center my weekly radio broadcast, "PrayerTime w/ Dr. Shelia", around the topic, "A 20/20 Self Focus". When this self-evaluating subject came to me, I had no idea what the entire world would be encountering in just a few months into 2020. The world was interrupted by the coronavirus, covid19, pandemic. God's Word reminds us that He is all knowing and He prepares us for what's to come. Although we didn't see the chaos of the pandemic coming, God was already working on our "Self-Focus" as 2020 began. He was reassuring us that staying focused on His promises and love would give us peace that reach way beyond our understanding. Unfortunately, many cannot see through the turbulence to siege these great opportunities that can be achieved. Instead of feeling encouraged, empowered, and fueled, some can only feel desperation, disappointment, and despair. Actually, when I began to write this book, an unbelievable level of unrest had already manifested. The early stages of the Covid19 pandemic had begun to unravel what was once normalcy and calmness like a tsunami making its way to an ocean's shore. Countries are still trying to maneuver their way through the seemingly endless maze of the effects of the devastation. Now, many have lost their lives, loved ones, jobs, means of income, homes, hope, faith, even their desire to live and survive. Unfortunately, giving up has seemed to become an option for some. Giving up cannot be an option. It is evident that an imperceptible sense of unrest and hopelessness are being experienced in some way. No matter what happens, hold on to the hope of God. Help is on the way! Time after time many have said and still are saying how irritated, bombarded, and overwhelmed they are with different chaotic situations. God can strengthen and send help and peace in the situation. Again I say, "Hold on, help is on the way". God's word says in Philippians 4:7-9

> *7 And the peace of God, which passeth all understanding, shall keep your hearts and minds through Christ Jesus.*
>
> *8 Finally, brethren, whatsoever things are true, whatsoever things are honest, whatsoever things are just, whatsoever things are pure, whatsoever things are lovely, whatsoever things are of good report; if there be any virtue, and if there be any praise, think on these things.*
> *9 Those things, which ye have both learned, and received, and heard, and seen in me, do: and the God of peace shall be with you.*

Even though racial tension and unlawful acts from different sectors have risen to another peak in history, some people are beginning to recognize the importance of love and togetherness. People are working together and lending a helping hand wherever needed. In 3 John 1:2 Paul was trying to encourage the brethren ``Beloved, I wish above all things that thou mayest prosper and be in health, even as thy soul prospereth". He was letting them know that they should be at peace with everything that would affect them. The brethren needed to stay faithful to God and the work of the ministry. John 10:10 is where Jesus said, "I have come that they may have life, and that they may have it more abundantly." If you are worried, edgy, or troubled about something in life, "precious one", start right now and relax your mind. Let go of all of the stress, and ask God to take control of the situation. He is able to bring peace to a troubled mind.

> *Isaiah 26:3 states "Thou wilt keep him in perfect peace, whose mind is stayed on thee: because he trusteth in thee".*

> *1 Peter 5:7, "Casting all your care upon him; for he careth for you."*

The purpose of this book is to help encourage, enlighten, and bring emphasis to the benefits of applying the Word of God to bring a sense of calmness in the middle of chaotic times. It will address some of the questions asked concerning the topic "The Calm in the Chaos"; Who? What? When? Where? Why? How? It will deal with the tension and stress of the seemingly unending trials of life in a biblical way to obtain the peace that surpasses all understanding. Even in the middle of pandemonic turmoil, we can experience peace, embrace opportunities, and enjoy the abundance of life. Let's journey together to gain knowledge in how to calm the chaos by applying the Word of God, prayer, and faith to our lives.

Opening Prayer

Heavenly Father we thank you for another day. We thank you for the ability to open our eyes and clothed in our right minds. We thank you for all that you have done and what you will continue to do, for we realize that without you we can do nothing. Lord we ask that you shield us with a hedge of protection as we go about our day. Lord we rebuke all weapons that are formed against us in our hearts, our minds, our souls, and our spirit in Jesus' name we pray Amen.

CHAPTER 1

CALM vs CHAOS

Daily challenges that could cause unrest and anxiety among individuals have increased. Healthy ways to navigate through the chaos of life must be accomplished. Is there any normalcy? Perhaps some cannot see any light of any normalcy, but staying calm, focused, and keeping a level head in the abnormal situations can be achieved. How to deal with those emotions that try to take control? The feeling one has can be the difference between peace and conflict, a relaxing evening and a nerve wrecking altercation, a peaceful sleep and a horrible nightmare. Fortunately, there are ways to face a chaotic situation and still maintain peace of mind and control of emotions.

There are some ways to relax in chaos. Taking deep breaths is one of the simplest ways to bring calmness to the body. When some people experience stress, they tend to breathe shallow and, often times, fast. Less oxygen for the blood or an elevated heart rate could be detrimental to the body, and stress chemicals would spike. Taking breaths restores the acceptable amount of oxygen needed to the body. Then, the body reacts and relaxes. Some people say that closing the eyes and blocking out distractions help too. Closing the eyes helps to regain focus, calms the breathing pattern, and helps muscles relax. It's ok to admit that something is causing stress. Don't give power to holding that stress in. Take the power to be calm back and deal with the stress head on. Then, find a way or create a plan to address the issues in a positive way. Find something to do, someone to talk to, or somewhere to go to take the mind off of the stress or chaos. Read the Word of God. It can be very helpful, comforting, encouraging, and relaxing. Listen to some uplifting music. Have quiet times of meditation. You can make it through this victoriously.

CHAPTER 2

WHO BRINGS CALM IN CHAOS?

GOD IS OUR REFUGE

What does it mean when someone says that God is a refuge? According to Webster-Merriam, refuge means "shelter or protection from danger or distress, a place that provides shelter or protection, or something to which one has recourse in difficulty". The Bible records at least 45 instances of depicting God as the refuge of safety and protection from harm and the storms of life. Knowing God as the only true safe place to be creates the ability to freely trust Him to protect in any situation. There is no need to fear people or spiritual attacks of the enemy when you are in the will of God. Nothing is too complicated for God to handle.

> *Proverbs 18:10 "The name of the LORD is a fortified tower; the righteous run to it and are safe".*

The protection and covering of God is available when sicknesses and diseases attack. He gives a place of safety under the shadow of His wings. God is the solidity of calmness in the midst of confusion. He is able to speedily rescue anyone who calls on Him. He is a faithful God. Psalm 62:8 gives an open invitation to all to "Trust in Him at all times, you people; pour out your hearts before Him". Why trust God and sincerely pour out the concerns of the heart to Him? God is faithful to His Word. He can and will rescue. Many times, God led the Israelites into wars where they were outnumbered and weaker than their adversaries. The Israelites found refuge in God's Word, trusted, and obeyed Him. Joshua and the Israelites, found in Joshua chapters 6 and 8, always came out with victory.

> *Psalms 91:1-7*
> *1 He that dwelleth in the secret place of the most High shall abide under the shadow of the Almighty. 2 I will say of the LORD, He is my refuge and my fortress: my God; in him will I trust. 3 Surely he shall deliver thee from the snare of the fowler, and from the noisome pestilence. 4 He shall cover thee with his feathers, and under his wings shalt thou trust: his truth shall be thy shield and buckler. 5 Thou shalt not be afraid for the terror by night; nor for the arrow that flieth by day; 6 Nor for the pestilence that walketh in darkness; nor for the destruction that wasteth at noonday. 7 A thousand shall fall at thy side, and ten thousand at thy right hand; but it shall not come nigh thee.*

THE LORD IS MY SHEPHERD

According to Spiritual Ray, 2020, Psalm 23 "The Lord is My Shepherd" is the most familiar and recited Psalm in the Bible. This passage of scripture narrates how loving and caring the Savior is towards His people, the sheep. It depicts how peaceful and satisfying it is to trust in Him and believe that the Good Shepherd can comfort and protect His own. Psalms 23 has been taught to many children throughout time. Perhaps, it was the first biblical scripture that a child recited by heart. Some read it to comfort at funerals. Some use it as a prayer to encourage others that His shielding presence is always available. He can take care of His own children. There is no lack or want for anything. The still waters portray the peace of God and carefree energy. Turbulent waters and waves signal complexities, lack of peace, worry, and difficulties. When the waters are still, it indicates stress-free and a peaceful feeling. It has been said that a sheep cannot survive without it's shepherd. Well, this is true spiritually too. Naturally, the sheep have no guidance on their own. They have no way to defend themselves. They are very fragile. The Lord is letting His sheep, the human race, know that they do not have to wander and possibly get destroyed by the enemy. The children of God need help to navigate through the rough places in life. They need someone to protect them from the devour. The good shepherd, the Lord and Savior Jesus Christ, living inside is a must. There is no need to be afraid when Christ is the forefront leading and guiding.

Psalms 23 The Lord is my shepherd; I shall not want.
² He maketh me to lie down in green pastures: he leadeth me beside the still waters.
³ He restoreth my soul: he leadeth me in the paths of righteousness for his name's sake.

⁴ Yea, though I walk through the valley of the shadow of death, I will fear no evil: for thou art with me; thy rod and thy staff they comfort me.
⁵ Thou preparest a table before me in the presence of mine enemies: thou anointest my head with oil; my cup runneth over.
⁶ Surely goodness and mercy shall follow me all the days of my life: and I will dwell in the house of the Lord forever.

JESUS CALMS THE STORM

Whatever the situation may be, the most safe and secure place to be is in the center of the Master's will and in His mighty arms of peace and protection. In John 16:33, Jesus told us, "In me you may have peace. In this world you will have trouble. But take heart! I have overcome the world". Hebrews 13:5–6 states, "Never will I leave you; never will I forsake you. So we say with confidence, The Lord is my helper; I will not be afraid. What can man do to me?" There were times that the disciples found themselves in some dangerous and difficult dilemmas. Jesus led the disciples into a boat. Jesus knew that a vicious storm would arise on their journey. While Jesus was confident in the power that worked in Him, the disciples were horrified and panicked. They were very upset with Jesus because He could sleep through the turbulence. The ship was being tossed around like a toy in a child's hand. Instead of understanding who Jesus really was and having faith, they got into their feelings and were terrified. They woke Jesus up to reprimand Him. They complained and accused Him of not caring for them and their safety. Someone right now, as you are reading this book, may be feeling that the Lord doesn't see the turmoil and feel the pain that you are experiencing or have experienced. Oh yes, He knows all things and He sees the struggles, feels the pain and sorrow, and He hears the cries. Jesus, their refuge, stood up and spoke to the wind. Instantly, the wind ceased. He calmed the violent storm and He can calm the raging storms that are pounding against your life and the entire world. Someone may be losing faith, but rest in the will of God. Face dangerous situations with confidence that the spoken Word of God can bring stillness to the raging waves of life.

> *Matthew 8:23-27 KJV*
> *And when he was entered into a ship, his disciples followed him. And, behold, there arose a great tempest in the sea, insomuch that the ship was covered with the waves: but he was asleep. And his disciples came to him, and awoke him, saying, Lord, save us: we perish. And he saith unto them, Why are ye fearful, O ye of little faith? Then he arose, and rebuked the winds and the sea; and there was a great calm. But the men marvelled, saying, What manner of man is this, that even the winds and the sea obey him!*

Regardless to the turmoil your personal storm may bring, I want you to be encouraged to know that nothing is as bad as it seems. According to Psalm 27:1-2, "The Lord is my light and my salvation; whom shall I fear? the Lord is the strength of my life; of whom shall I be afraid? 2 When the wicked, even mine enemies and my foes, came upon me to eat up my flesh, they stumbled and fell." In the middle of your hardest times in life, turn to the Word of God and allow it to minister to your spirit. Do not be afraid of the storms of life, but depend on God's Word to help you make the necessary decisions to give you peace.

CHAPTER 3

HOW TO WEATHER A STORM

This topic was part of the Pre Covid19 message on my radio broadcast, "PrayerTime w/ Dr. Shelia". I didn't know at the time of the broadcast that the entire world was about to experience such chaos that has never been witnessed before simultaneously in history. Every country was beginning to face an unimaginable sense of panic, grief, fear, and disbelief. For months, a horrific storm, the Pandemic, had been brewing that would change every individual's life in one way or another. Fortunately, alerts are given when natural storms are coming so we can begin to prepare for it, but life's storms can hit us by surprise. Oftentimes, these sudden unannounced storms cause hardship and severe damage to our lives.

TROUBLES

Today, many people are experiencing some turbulent storms in their lives. Pandemonium and different kinds of chaotic troubles unexpectedly hit the entire world and triggered a wrenching, domino effect result. Unfortunately, no one was prepared for the massive and destructive aftermath. Many are still suffering with pain and hurt from this unannounced whirlwind of disaster. When the storms of life come, they can cause our lives to change forever. So, solutions are needed to know how to prepare for and weather these tumultuous events and how to bounce back from the damage that occurs from life's storms. It is important to go to God for safety. We should learn God's Word and stand on the promises of help in troublesome times.

> *[28] Then they cry unto the Lord in their trouble, and he bringeth them out of their distresses.[29] He maketh the storm a calm, so that the waves thereof are still.[30] Then are they glad because they be quiet; so he bringeth them unto their desired haven.*

This chapter is not talking about weather in noun sense but as a verb. How is someone going to survive or get through these storms? One thing that is for sure is that trouble will come in life to disrupt the normal flow of things. Troubles sometimes cannot be avoided. The Bible clearly states in Job 14:1, "Man that is born of a woman is of few days and full of trouble". People do not have to have done anything wrong for storms to wreak havoc in their lives. Job was a man who always tried to please God. He was also wealthy. He had many possessions. Psalms 34:19 says, "Many are the afflictions of the righteous: but the LORD delivereth him out of them all".

> *Psalm 34:17-20*
> *[17]The righteous cry, and the LORD heareth, and delivereth them out of all their troubles. [18]The LORD is nigh unto them that are of a broken heart; and saveth such as be of a contrite spirit. [19]Many are*

the afflictions of the righteous: but the LORD delivereth him out of them all. 20He keepeth all his bones: not one of them is broken.

DON'T GIVE UP!

Daylight may not be seen immediately but do not give up for the darkest hour is just before dawn. The present struggles are as real as the sun is hot. The Word of God said that the righteous would experience many afflictions, but the Lord would rescue us from every one of them.

Isaiah 54:10 ^{10} For the mountains shall depart, and the hills be removed; but my kindness shall not depart from thee, neither shall the covenant of my peace be removed, saith the Lord that hath mercy on thee.

Psalms 46:1-6
46 God is our refuge and strength, a very present help in trouble.
^{2} Therefore will not we fear, though the earth be removed, and though the mountains be carried into the midst of the sea;
^{3} Though the waters thereof roar and be troubled, though the mountains shake with the swelling thereof. Selah.
^{4} There is a river, the streams whereof shall make glad the city of God, the holy place of the tabernacles of the most High.
^{5} God is in the midst of her; she shall not be moved: God shall help her, and that right early.
^{6} The heathen raged, the kingdoms were moved: he uttered his voice, the earth melted

Yes, the struggles of life are real, but God has assured His children that it is possible to make it through them. Continue to have faith. One may say, "How is it possible to have faith when everything around me seems to be collapsing before my eyes?" I didn't say that it was an easy thing to do. Sometimes, talking with someone and thinking of happy times will help a person to get one step closer to a moment of peace. Every day won't be the same. Read God's Word, especially Romans 8:27-28. He already knows that weariness has set in and pain is in the hearts of His children. Cry out to Him and trust Him to make a way in these dark days and stand on His Word.

> *27 And he that searcheth the hearts knoweth what is the mind of the Spirit, because he maketh intercession for the saints according to the will of God.*
> *28 And we know that all things work together for good to them that love God, to them who are the called according to his purpose.*

Romans 8:38-39 "For I am sure that neither death nor life, nor angels nor rulers, nor things present nor things to come, nor powers, nor height nor depth, nor anything else in all creation, will be able to separate us from the love of God in Christ Jesus our Lord."

Don't' Give Up Checklist

- Thank God for Life the moment you open your eyes in the morning.
- Ask the Spirt of God to help you to make clear, conscious decisions.

- Give yourself credit. Reflect on this daily, "You are fearfully and wonderfully made after God's image. (Psalm 139:14)" With God's help, you can make it!
- Start your own private journal of your thoughts and gratitude. Keep first things first and stay on track.
- Repeat this throughout the day, "I am more than a conqueror (Romans 8:37) and I can do all things through Christ which strengthens me."(Philippians 4:13) Believe it!

CHAPTER 4

TURNING STRUGGLES INTO SUCCESS

Coping with the uncertainties of difficult times, one must always realize that nothing or no one is perfect. The joyous, happy, and celebrated times of life occur and we celebrate them. Unfortunately, the difficult, sad, and almost unbearable times happen too. Life's difficulties happen. Sometimes bad things happen unexpectedly and are very hard to deal with. Individuals won't get it right every time. Sometimes, we may think negatively and wrong. We must accept the fact that valleys are a part of getting to the mountain top. Once we grasp the reality of low times and realize that they are only temporary, then, we can begin to shift the mindset into a more positive direction. Getting through and rising above the turbulent moments in life can begin to take place. Without the help of the Lord, failure and disappointments can happen. No one should conclude that failure is the end result. Strive to survive and succeed. Do not accept or give in to defeat. It is necessary to examine and determine whether or not the trouble and trials in front of us are bigger than the hope of a good ending. If a meltdown occurs, it's ok only for a very short second. Just don't melt away into depression and anxiety. God already knows that it has gotten too much to bear. Talk to Him. Ask for strength and guidance through the problems in your life. Then, trust God to send help in your time of distress. Shake yourself off, get back on track and become stronger from the setbacks. It doesn't matter what is happening in or around your life. Keep fighting for the prize of success and accomplish happiness and peace. God promised these treasures to us, peace, joy, and happiness.

FRUSTRATED BUT MOTIVATED

Have you ever heard the phrase, "When it rains it pours". Well, it may just happen to pour sometimes in our lives, but the downpour doesn't have to drown us. Maybe things right now are not how we expected them to be. Maybe we are not at the place in life that we intended or projected to be. So what! We can get back on course with a change of attitude about our unwelcomed misfortunes and navigate around the stumbling blocks and still come out victorious. Undoubtedly, difficulties and seemingly insurmountable hardships have caused dark clouds to hover over our lives. The darkness has definitely affected outlooks on life and our emotions. Believe it or not, we can use the frustration that we are experiencing to motivate us to push through the pain and anguish and move forward in our mind and spirit. See your frustration as a catapult not a heavy weight to your place of success that you desire to achieve. There is promise in this pandemic and time of global unrest. This may look like it's not going in your favor but hang in there, things will work out in your favor.

Psalms 5:12 Surely, LORD, you bless the righteous; you surround them with your favor as with a shield.

1 Peter 5:7⁷ Casting all your care upon him; for he careth for you.

Proverbs 15:22 "Without counsel plans fail, but with many advisers they succeed."

Romans 8:31-32 "What then shall we say to these things? If God is for us, who can be against us? He who did not spare his own Son but gave him up for us all, how will he not also with him graciously give us all things?"

POSITIVE THINKING

Often times, we can become impatient and discouraged because things are not going well in our lives. Remaining focused and remembering that anything worth having will take time to possess. .A lot has transpired in our lives. Adjusting to change takes time. When faced with adversities, we must allow ourselves the ability to shift positively. We have been challenged greatly to adjusting to a new normal, a new way of doing things, and a new way of thinking and handling our lives. Shifting to the unknown is not always an easy transition. The greatest challenge is admitting that things have changed. Therefore, the change possibly requires a different approach in order to come out victoriously.

> *Matthew 17:20*
> *And Jesus said unto them, Because of your unbelief: for verily I say unto you, If ye have faith as a grain of mustard seed, ye shall say unto this mountain, Remove hence to yonder place; and it shall remove; and nothing shall be impossible unto you.*

Trying to learn or do something different can be frightening. By accepting that things are different and adjusting to the abnormity could decrease long term anxiety and possible future failures. Focus on one day at a time. Make plans but don't dwell too hard on tomorrow. The Bible tells us that God will supply our needs from day to day. Stay positive and stay focused and on course to the greatest success imaginable to you. Negativity will cheat you out of knowing and benefiting from the greater lesson learned in every trial.

> *Philippians 4:8*
> *8Finally, brethren, whatsoever things are true, whatsoever things are honest, whatsoever things are just, whatsoever things are pure, whatsoever things are lovely, whatsoever things are of good report; if there be any virtue, and if there be any praise, think on these things. 9Those things, which ye have both learned, and received, and heard, and seen in me, do: and the God of peace shall be with you.*

Philippians 4:19
But my God shall supply all your need according to his riches in glory by Christ Jesus.

Matthew 6:25-34

25Therefore I say unto you, Take no thought for your life, what ye shall eat, or what ye shall drink; nor yet for your body, what ye shall put on. Is not the life more than meat, and the body than raiment? 26Behold the fowls of the air: for they sow not, neither do they reap, nor gather into barns; yet your heavenly Father feedeth them. Are ye not much better than they? 27Which of you by taking thought can add one cubit unto his stature? 28And why take ye thought for raiment? Consider the lilies of the field, how they grow; they toil not, neither do they spin: 29And yet I say unto you, That even Solomon in all his glory was not arrayed like one of these. 30Wherefore, if God so clothe the grass of the field, which today is, and to-morrow is cast into the oven, shall he not much more clothe you, O ye of little faith? 31Therefore take no thought, saying, What shall we eat? or, What shall we drink? or, Wherewithal shall we be clothed? 32(For after all these things do the Gentiles seek:) for your heavenly Father knoweth that ye have need of all these things. 33But seek ye first the kingdom of God, and his righteousness; and all these things shall be added unto you. 34Take therefore no thought for the morrow: for the morrow shall take thought for the things of itself. Sufficient unto the day is the evil thereof.

In order to be successful in times of struggle, it is mandatory that you receive positive energy from others around you, and you give out positive energy to the ones around "you". Practicing positivity will definitely be evident of an inward healing to the people around you. Make a conscious decision to be more positive during these times of disparities. Your way of thinking will affect how you feel and how you act. Avoid, at all cost, complaining people with a negative mindset. Negativity would dampen your spirit and invade your mindset and peace. Focus on the good that is happening or anticipated. Appreciate what you have now, and embrace what is working for you. Trust God's Word, and the rest will turn out favorable for you.

CHAPTER 5

WHEN WE ALL PRAY TOGETHER

What can really happen when all of God's children pray with sincerity and in unity? Chaos and disturbances would have to flee. Blinded eyes would open, the lame would walk, and the dumb would talk. Death, depression, anger, hate, financial burdens, suicide, and everything else that would cause distress and pain would have to go in the name of Jesus.

> *Acts 12:5-11*
> *⁵ Peter therefore was kept in prison: but prayer was made without ceasing of the church unto God for him.*
> *⁶ And when Herod would have brought him forth, the same night Peter was sleeping between two soldiers, bound with two chains: and the keepers before the door kept the prison.*
> *⁷ And, behold, the angel of the Lord came upon him, and a light shined in the prison: and he smote Peter on the side, and raised him up, saying, Arise up quickly. And his chains fell off from his hands.*
> *⁸ And the angel said unto him, Gird thyself, and bind on thy sandals. And so he did. And he saith unto him, Cast thy garment about thee, and follow me.*

⁹ And he went out, and followed him; and wist not that it was true which was done by the angel; but thought he saw a vision.

¹⁰ When they were past the first and the second ward, they came unto the iron gate that leadeth unto the city; which opened to them of his own accord: and they went out, and passed on through one street; and forthwith the angel departed from him.

¹¹ And when Peter was come to himself, he said, Now I know of a surety, that the Lord hath sent his angel, and hath delivered me out of the hand of Herod, and from all the
expectation of the people of the Jews.

When we all pray together, what could happen? Yes, we all "can" pray the Word of God together in unity. Supernatural things can happen. The Word of God tells us about praying and seeking his face. I want to elaborate briefly about praying together in this chapter. I do believe that prayer changes things. You may have a situation in your life, and you feel as though there is no hope. I want you to turn to the God who is willing and able to be a present help in your time of trouble.

Psalm 46:1-3 — "God is our refuge and strength, an ever-present help in trouble. Therefore we will not fear, though the earth give way and the mountains fall into the heart of the sea, though its waters roar and foam and the mountains quake with their surging."

Psalm 46:8-11 — "Come and see what the Lord has done, the desolations He has brought on the earth. He makes wars cease to the ends of the earth. He breaks the bow and shatters the spear; He burns the shields with fire. He says, "Be still, and know that I am God; I will be exalted among the nations, I will be exalted in the earth." The Lord Almighty is with us; the God of Jacob is our fortress."

Hebrews 4:14-16 — "Since then we have a great high priest who has passed through the heavens, Jesus, the Son of God, let us hold fast our confession. For we do not have a high priest who is unable to sympathize with our weaknesses, but one who in every respect has been tempted as we are, yet without sin. Let us then with confidence draw near to the throne of grace, that we may receive mercy and find grace to help in time of need."

MIRACLES CAN HAPPEN!

First, I want you to praise God right now for the things that He has already done. When we pray together, miracles can happen. You know, it reminds me of a situation that was happening in Acts 12: 3-19 when Peter was put in Jail by King Herod. The bible says that constant prayers were offered up unto God. In the fifth verse of chapter 12, "Peter therefore was kept in prison, prayer without ceasing was made of the church unto God" for him. Yes, prayer was made. That means there were some people who got together and prayed nonstop for their fellow man. They could not physically go in and break him out, but their prayers caused a supernatural, spiritual breakout or release. In the Word of God, it said they prayed without ceasing. There is no doubt that they had daily chores to do, but they knew the power of unified prayers. They came together in corporate prayer, praise, and worship. Life does not stop when tragedy hits you in the face. Never stop praying and giving God praise for the things that He promised He would do. God is not short concerning His promises. 2 Peter 3:9 says, "The Lord is not slack concerning his promise, as some men count slackness; but is longsuffering to us-ward, not willing that any should perish, but that all should come to repentance." At the same time chaos and unimaginable turbulence is wreaking havoc in your life, you can and should have a mindset of focusing on the things of God by applying the Word of God. You can still be in a state of Prayer and peace of mind. These people were together in their spirit with one agenda, to petition God for Peter's safety and release. The Word of God said the church was praying to God without ceasing and giving thanks to God, 1 Thessalonian 5:17-18. As they were sending their prayers forth, the angel came inside the jail. Peter was bound by his hand and feet. The guards were to watch him and make sure that he was not going anywhere. But my God, through effectual fervent prayers, had another plan. The angel told him to rise, put on your sandals and let us go. Immediately the chains fell off. It does not take God long to do anything. Do not stop praying and believing that God will show up mightily in your situation. Peter thought he was having a vision. Sometimes, when God performs miraculously in our lives, we wonder if it is real. That is the power of prayer. Sometimes, you do not have to physically do anything but pray and have faith. Sometimes, we think that if we do not hurry up and do something about it ourselves physically, people are going to run over us. Sometimes we may think that we are going to lose this or that. We must keep ourselves focused on God and lift that problem, that situation up in prayer. Now, when you lift that situation up in prayer, expect God to move on that petition. Prayer is not only a tool, but it is also something to defend and defeat the enemies. That angel came in and Peter walked right out. Peter was so shocked. He thought it was a dream. When Peter and the angel got up to the gate, do you know what the Word says happened? The gate miraculously swung open on its own. What a mighty God we serve! When Peter came to himself, he said, "Now I know of a surety that God had sent His angel and delivered me out of the hands of Herod and from the expectation of the Jewish people". Then, he went where the people of God were praying for him. Yes, they were diligently praying for him. Sometimes, we are like Peter. We know that God is right there for us, but when we are in the middle of our trials, that situation becomes overwhelming. We still need to remain faithful to His Word and promises. God said that He would never leave us nor forsake us.

> *Deuteronomy 31:8 -The Lord himself goes before you and will be with you; he will never leave you nor forsake you. Do not be afraid; do not be discouraged.*

We must be determined to hold on and trust God with everything within us. Regardless of how the enemy tries to bring stumbling blocks in our lives, it does not matter, because when God gets ready to move, He's going to move in your favor. We must continue to stay prayerful and do His Will. We cannot talk negatively. If we talk negatively, we will allow the devil to come in and steal our joy and steal our victory. It is crucial that we do not allow negative talk and negative influences around us, especially during the time that we are going through trials and tribulation. Connect with Spirit filled individuals who will help you and fervently pray for you without ceasing. They will be with one accord with you. Be encouraged in knowing that God is going to move on your behalf. Keep praying! Do not give up! Your breakthrough is coming!

> *Psalm 91:14-16 (God) – "Because he holds fast to me in love, I will deliver him; I will protect him, because he knows my name. When he calls to me, I will answer him; I will be with him in trouble; I will rescue him and honour him. With long life I will satisfy him and show him my salvation."*
> *Psalm 18:6-19 – "In my distress I called upon the Lord; to my God I cried for help. From His temple he heard my voice, and my cry to Him reached His ears.*

Until He moves, enjoy life and pray always. Watch God move. Praying together is an individual decision corporately weaving us together. We are worth taking care of one another, praying, and fasting for one another. There is nothing like having that personal relationship with God. Also, if two of us can agree on anything, God said that He would be right there in that situation.

Matthew 18:19-20
19 Again I say unto you, That if two of you shall agree on earth as touching anything that they shall ask, it shall be done for them of my Father which is in heaven. 20 For where two or three are gathered together in my name, there am I in the midst of them.

Sometimes we may have anxiety in our heart. Anxiety occurs when a person is overtaken by the mere thought of what might happen. The situation may not have even occurred. Surround yourself with people who are true prayer warriors who know how to pray. God Word says in Proverbs 21 that the heart of the king is in the hand of the Lord, and He moves like the water. God knows how to stir the water regardless of what is going on in your life. Your water of life may be sickness, pain, depression, loss of finances, loss of a loved one, anxiety, etc. Whatever the problem is, you must give it to God in Prayer. God has the power to do the impossible. We must learn to apply the Word of God in any and every situation.

GOD IS WAITING ON YOU TO SURRENDER

Never think that you should face troubling situations alone. There is nothing too small or too big for God. Your Heavenly Father is extremely interested in what you are going through. I have heard some people say that "It is my business and I do not need anyone to

tell me what to do" or "I can handle this by myself".
My brothers and sisters, God does not want you to go
through these terrible times alone. He is right there
listening for you to cry out to Him. He loves His
people. He is waiting to heal us everywhere we hurt.
We cannot have a stiff neck or a stubborn spirit. Just
be humble and let God know that you cannot take
this journey alone. Let Him know how you really feel.
God already knows exactly where you are and how
much you can bear. He's waiting to hear from you.

> *2 Chronicles 7:12-15*
> *12 the Lord appeared to him at night and said:*
> *"I have heard your prayer and have chosen this place*
> *for myself as a temple for sacrifices. 13 "When I*
> *shut up the heavens so that there is no rain, or*
> *command locusts to devour the land or send a plague*
> *among my people, 14 if my people, who are called by*
> *my name, will humble themselves and pray and seek*
> *my face and turn from their wicked ways, then I will*
> *hear from heaven, and I will forgive their sin and*
> *will heal their land. 15 Now my eyes will be open*
> *and my ears attentive to the prayers offered in this*
> *place.*

1 Corinthians 10:13 says, "There hath no temptation
taken you but such as is common to man: but God is
faithful, who will not suffer you to be tempted above
that ye are able; but will with the temptation also
make a way to escape, that ye may be able to bear it".
Pray and ask God to send you someone to pray and
intercede for you. "The effectual fervent prayer of a
righteous man availeth much", according to James
5:16. The word fervent suggests the concept of

"stimulating or energizing," like an electric current that generates power to a circuit. When used in this passage of scripture, fervent implies a kind of prayer that is "fiery, heartfelt, intense, insistent, and unrelenting". All of us need someone who is in our corner, as the elders used to say, "can get a prayer through", lifting us up before the Lord. You do not need to be alone. Jesus was talking to Simon and told him that He had been praying for him. Jesus knew that Simon Peter was about to be faced with something so great that he would deny Jesus and say that he was not one of His disciples.

> *Luke 22:31-34*
> *31 "Satan hath desired to have you , that he may sift you as wheat,: 32 But I prayed for you that your faith fail not: and when thou are converted, strengthen thy brother.*

My sister, my brother, be strong in the Lord and continue to pray and be your brother's keeper. Pray sincerely for one another. When we all began to pray together for the Will of God through His Word, this whole world could be affected. Changes could occur. Souls could be saved, set free, and delivered. We could witness and experience supernatural miracles in our lives and the lives of others.

CHAPTER 6

STOMPING OUT THE ENEMY

We as children of God, we can overcome any problem with Christ, great or small. No prayer is too hard for Him to answer. Three hundred sixty-five times the admonition, "Fear Not," is stated in the Bible. Amazingly, there is a "Fear Not" for every day of the year. There are numerous things happening in this world to cause us to feel afraid. On the other hand, Biblically, there are many promises of protection and peace to increase our faith to calm our fears. Jesus didn't promise us that He would be with us **some** days. He promised to stay with us always, even unto the end of the age, Matthew 28:20.

> *Deuteronomy 31:6-8*
> *"Be strong and courageous. Do not fear or be in dread of them, for it is the LORD your God who goes with you. He will not leave you or forsake you." Then Moses summoned Joshua and said to him in the sight of all Israel, "Be strong and courageous, for you shall go with this people into the land that the LORD has sworn to their fathers to give them, and you shall put them in possession of it. It is the LORD who goes before you. He will be with you; he will not leave you or forsake you. Do not fear or be dismayed."*

FAITH OVER FEAR

As I have previously stated, the entire world seemingly full of trouble, despair and uncertainty. It can be very easy to feel overcome with fear. It can be very hard not to be fearful and disturbed. Heartbreakingly, many have lost any glimpse of hope. We must choose faith in God's Word and His promises over fear. If you're feeling overwhelmed and want to overcome the fears of today, it's important that you are confident in God and His Word. The way to become confident, we must study His Word. Hear His voice and obey His instructions. Many of the people in the Bible faced obstacles that caused them to become fearful, but fear did not prevail. They overcame it through faith, trust, and believing the almighty God. Abraham and Sarah waited for the promised child that God told them that they would have.

Genesis 18:10-15
10Then one of them said, "I will surely return to you about this time next year, and Sarah your wife will have a son."

Now Sarah was listening at the entrance to the tent, which was behind him. 11Abraham and Sarah were already very old, and Sarah was past the age of childbearing. 12So Sarah laughed to herself as she thought, "After I am worn out and my lord is old, will I now have this pleasure?"

13Then the Lord said to Abraham, "Why did Sarah laugh and say, 'Will I really have a child, now that I am old?' 14Is anything too hard for the Lord?

I will return to you at the appointed time next year, and Sarah will have a son."

15Sarah was afraid, so she lied and said, "I did not laugh."

But he said, "Yes, you did laugh."

The Isaac Promise did not come when they wanted it. They even doubted that God would do what He said. In their old age and against the odds, God showed up and proved Himself mighty. Do not be afraid when it looks dim as though nothing is going to work out. Yes, it may look like everything's falling apart and everybody is unhinged. Thankfully, God is much more powerful than the evil forces that are coming against you. Some of us are afraid that we're going to die, be homeless, hungry, broke, jobless, sick, etc. Some just do not believe that they are going to come out of their struggles right now. Hold on to God's Word for Psalm 145:13 says, "The Lord is faithful to all his promises and loving toward all he has made."

POWER OF GOD

When our future seems uncertain, how can we trust God's omnipotent power to rescue us from the spirit of fear and the many troubles we face daily? Let me explain the word, "omnipotent". According to Merriam-Webster, omnipotent means having unlimited power and/or influence. It is also referenced like this, GOD, all caps. Luke 1:37 says, For nothing will be impossible with God. Knowing, believing, and experiencing the power of God in the midst of all of the crises is vital to our total victory.

Jeremiah 32:26-27 clearly reassures us that there is nothing that is too hard for God to do for us; "Then came the word of the LORD unto Jeremiah, saying Behold, I *am* the LORD, the God of all flesh: Is there anything too hard for me?" What a mighty God we serve!
He is omnipotent in creation. He spoke and creation began to evolve from nothing to life.

> *Isaiah 44:24 "This is what the LORD says—your Redeemer, who formed you in the womb: I am the LORD, the Maker of all things, who stretches out the heavens, who spreads out the earth by myself."*

God has all power concerning the salvation of mankind. God sent His only Son, His Word in the flesh to give us hope and a future with Him.

> *Jude 24-25 "To him who is able to keep you from stumbling and to present you before his glorious presence without fault and with great joy—to the only God our Savior be glory, majesty, power and authority, through Jesus Christ our Lord, before all ages, now and forevermore! Amen."*

God is all powerful in the Resurrection of His Son Jesus Christ for redemption of our sins and reconciles us back to Him.

> *John 10:17-18 – "The reason my Father loves me is that*

I lay down my life—only to take it up again. No one takes it from me, but I lay it down of my own accord. I have authority to lay it down and authority to take it up again. This command I received from my Father."

God is all powerful and limitless in His understanding of our infirmities and trials. He knows our sorrows. He hears our cry and supplications. He is not ignoring us.

Psalm 147:5 "Great is our Lord and mighty in power; his understanding has no limit."

We have to choose faith in God and not fear of the enemy. Yes, the crises seem big and life-threatening. Many Christians say that they trust God's will for their lives, but they are not willing to let go of the doubt and fear. I truly believe that God has a supernatural relief plan and purpose for us, if we can keep the faith. There is no doubt that most Christians do not have an issue in believing this. The issue is that we cannot seem to override the carnal nature of mankind and let God work it out His way, not our way. When His plan or way does not coincide with our idea or plan, that's when our carnal mind began to conjure up doubts and fear; allowing our own desires disregard the plan of God.

2 Timothy 1:7[7] For God hath not given us the spirit of fear; but of power, and of love, and of a sound mind.

Isaiah 41:13¹³ For I the Lord thy God will hold thy right hand, saying unto thee, Fear not; I will help thee.

God has the power to help you and me at the same time. He is everywhere, all over this world at the same time. He is omnipresent. Our confidence in the power of God should be enhanced by now. As a matter of fact, God's Word in many passages of the scripture encourages us to rely on Him for help.

> *Isaiah 65:34, "And it shall come to pass, that before they call, I will answer; and while they are yet speaking, I will hear. There is not a need that He can't supply. There is not a sickness, disease, pain, or hurt that He can't heal. He is able to deliver us out of all of our afflictions. He is All powerful. We can't do anything without Him. Through His Son, we are more than conquerors.*

> *Philippians 4:13 says, "I can do all this through him who gives me strength."*

> *Jude 1:24 "Now unto him that is able to keep you from falling, and to present you faultless before the presence of his glory with exceeding joy,"*

> *Ephesians 3:20-21 Now unto him that is able to do exceeding abundantly above all that we ask or think, according to the power that worketh in us,*

> *21 Unto him be glory in the church by Christ Jesus throughout all ages, world without end. Amen.*

43

LOVE

There is one thing that can "cast out fear" and that is the power of love. Love demonstrated can encourage even the "lowest in spirit" individual. It can cause the depressed to regain hope in hopeless times. Love can make someone who is fearful to believe that true strength lies within. Fear can be conquered. You may ask, "How?" The more you know and understand the power of love, the less fear can occupy that space in your mind. Sometimes, fear is given the power to control us because we may lack or have limited true knowledge of God's promises in the Bible or lack of faith in His promises and power.

> *1 John 4:18.*
> *"There is no fear in love; but perfect love casteth out fear: because fear hath torment. He that feareth is not made perfect in love."*

There are ways to increase your faith and conquer your fears. For instance, a child who is afraid of the dark can overcome fear when the mother implements her loving touch and soft words of assurance that everything is going to be alright. That child knows that mother loves and protects, so fear becomes less or even goes away. Our Father loves us with such a compassionate love. He protects us. When we choose to love God, accept Him as the One who has power over everything and have faith in Him, we have no need to be enslaved by fear, uncertainties, and superstitious encounters. Did you know that there are abnormal fears that can grip the mind and emotions send them into an anxiety overload? Some abnormal fears may be the fear of health failure when you are not sick; Fear of losing your job; Fear of dying; etc. If we can truly believe to the point of knowing that God is concerned about our well-being, we can trust in our Father's Agape love towards us. He is a loving and concerned Father. He loves and cares for us. He sent His son Jesus to pay the sin ransom for us. Thank you my loving Father. Surely, He will take us through these trying times to a victorious outcome.

SOUND MIND

We must make a conscious decision to just say " I am going to give it to God and trust Him at His Word." He promised that He would not leave us nor forsake us. Unfortunately, after the announcement of Covid-19, many people's minds were very distorted and discombobulated. Some were scrambling to find any word of assurance and guidance to how to navigate through this attack of the unknown enemy. Some found comfort in the Word of God and His promises to us. Our times are in God's hands, and nothing can overtake us apart from His permission. We must exercise a moment-by-moment trust in an all-knowing Lord. We must maintain an unshakable faith and belief that God has everything under control, and that nothing can harm us beyond God's plan, because we are constantly moving under the shadow of the Almighty. We need to learn to exchange our fears for a simple childlike trust.

1 Corinthians 15:58 Therefore, my beloved brethren, be ye steadfast, unmovable, always abounding in the work of the Lord, forasmuch as ye know that your labour is not in vain in the Lord.

Joshua 1:9 ⁹ Have not I commanded thee? Be strong and of a good courage; be not afraid, neither be thou dismayed: for the Lord thy God is with thee whithersoever thou goest.

Isaiah 41:10
¹⁰ Fear thou not; for I am with thee: be not dismayed; for I am thy God: I will strengthen thee; yea, I will help thee; yea, I will uphold thee with the right hand of my righteousness.

CHAPTER 7

LEAN AND DEPEND ON GOD

To attempt to avoid fear could rob us of an in depth experience of the measure of faith that has been given to us. In order to choose faith over fear, confidence and trust in God and His Word are critical. Reading, learning, hearing, understanding, and applying the scriptures of God's Word would strengthen our faith. Also, we can begin to learn how to lean and depend on God. The Bible is intended to help us make sense of the overwhelming chaos and uncertainties that surround us. We see people overtaken in fear of contracting Coronavirus and dying from it or fear of dying at the hands of someone. We have a strong and powerful God who can hold us all at the same time. No matter how you feel, lean on Him. He is able to keep you from falling down and giving in. You cannot see Him with the physical eye. Oh, but you can feel His sweet presence all around you. Just lift those hands of yours right where you are and repeat after me these words.

"Father God, I don't have the answers but I am trusting you to hold me up and keep me from giving up. I don't really understand why and I don't know how, so I am leaning and depending on what your

Word says to me. I am acknowledging you as my Lord and Savior. I believe. I give these troubles all to you in the name of Jesus. Philippians 4:6, "Do not be anxious about anything, but in every situation, by prayer and petition, with thanksgiving, present your requests to God." Therefore, I am praying to you with everything that's within me. I realize that I am not able to do this alone. I need your strong and mighty hand to help me. Thank you Lord for your forgiveness, love, and sacrifice. Amen

It is important to know that God commissions us each and every day to simply trust and have faith in Him in every area in our lives. Even though things can get extremely difficult to endure, we must continue to move forward. It is not good to worry about tomorrow's unknown happenings. Even some Christians engage in the battle in the mind between trust and the spirit of fear. Whatever name we may attach it to such as: worrying, anxiety, paranoia, etc. none of these are healthy to the body, mind, or spirit. Our emotional health, mental health, and physical health can reach a "fear overload capacity" and give room to depression. Depression can be that deadly weapon to attack and make even a healthy person gravely ill. It is possible to lose sight of the peace of God and happiness that He promised us. Refuse to worry. Pray and stand on God's word.

Psalms 37:5 Commit thy way unto the Lord; trust also in him; and he shall bring it to pass.

Psalms 37:25 I have been young, and now am old; yet have I not seen the righteous forsaken, nor his seed begging bread.

John 14:1 Let not your heart be troubled: ye believe in God, believe also in me.

Psalm 37:23 "The steps of a man are established by the Lord, when he delights in his way."

TALK TO THE LORD

God is always available and waiting for us to talk to Him. He is the God of every kind of comfort. He is able to give us peace. Do not be afraid to communicate with Him. When you talk to Him, picture God as your friend. That is who He is. Just surrender your will and plans unto Him and let Him work on your behalf.

Proverb 3:5-6 Trust in the Lord with all your heart and lean not on your own understanding; 6 in all your ways submit to him, and he will make your paths straight.

2 Corinthians 1:3 "Blessed be the God and Father of our Lord Jesus Christ, the Father of mercies and God of all comfort."

Do not try to figure the answer out. Our way or our understanding may not be His way. God is able to direct your path and make it easier for you to maneuver through this pathway called Life. God has a sweet, listening ear. You may not know what to say. It's ok, because He knows what you need. Meditate on God's promises and biblical principles. Keep the faith and trust Him. He is your GPS.

> *Romans 8:34 Who then is the one who condemns? No one. Christ Jesus who died-more than that, who was raised to life-is at the right hand of God and is also interceding for us.*

SEEK WISE COUNSEL

David was faced with the loss of his family and all of his soldiers' family. His men were ready to kill him. He was in a very difficult place as a leader. He remembered to consult the Lord concerning how he should handle this tragedy. God answered with authority and told him to go after the enemies, and assured him that he would recover everything. In these trying times, God is going to give us the ability to recover all. Thank you Lord for victory!

> *1 Samuel 30:6-8 6David was desperate. His soldiers were so upset over what had happened to their sons and daughters that they were thinking about stoning David to death. But he felt the LORD God giving him strength, 7 and he said to the priest, "Abiathar, let's ask God what to do."*
> *Abiathar brought everything he needed to get answers from God, and he went over to David. 8Then David asked the LORD, "Should I go after*

the people who raided our town? Can I catch up with them?"

"Go after them," the LORD answered. "You will catch up with them, and you will rescue your families."

David sought the priest. He had confidence in the priest. First thing we need to do is pray and ask God to send us the right people as counselors. The person should have a strong personal relationship with God. The person needs to be truthful, knows how to talk to God and hear from God. A mentor/counselor needs to be very knowledgeable in every way, especially in the Word of God. The person needs to have God-like character, experience, compassion, integrity, discernment, wisdom, kindness, strategy and a good reputation. Pray and ask God to send you the right person to help you navigate through your battles.

> *Proverbs 12:26 "The righteous choose their friends carefully, but the way of the wicked leads them astray".*

> *Proverbs 1:5 "Let the wise listen and add to their learning, and let the discerning get guidance".*

CHAPTER 8

RISING TO THE CHALLENGE

David, in 1 Samuel chapters 16-19, is an excellent example of someone who knew how to talk to God. Even as a little shepherd boy, he was able to follow God's guidance. He was one who did not allow fear to overtake him. He fought the lion and rescued the sheep out of its mouth, fought a bear and saved the sheep, and even killed the fierce giant, Goliath, with a slingshot and a smooth rock. He rose to the challenge as a small boy, because he knew who God is and the power He possesses. We must confront the giants in our lives. Fear of defeat may be that Goliath that you run from every time adversities come. David did not look at the statue of Goliath neither was he afraid of his loud voice spewing out threats and insults. He had experienced the rescuing power of God in the fields tending his father's sheep. He had confidence in his God. I say to you, "Do not let the loud noises of your Goliath intimidate you. God is all powerful.

Romans 8:37 "We are more than conquerors through him who loved us."

To conquer is to be triumphant over an opponent. To be "more than a conqueror" implies that we do not just attain victory, but we are extraordinarily victorious. You can recover all. Rise up and fight!

FIGHTING TO ENDURE

We need power outside of ourselves. Do not be too proud or afraid to ask for strength to endure and power to conquer. David needed power, strength, and help on numerous occasions during the course of his life. He definitely was not too proud to ask for it. He, as a king, consulted God for power to fight in battles and the ability to endure and come out victoriously. He was not too proud to admit he needed help. He said in Psalm 42:2, "My soul thirsteth for God, for the living God:" David is known as "the man who is after God's own heart". That speaks volume. To have the ability to move God intimately and passionately like David did is a powerful precious gift. In Psalm 27:1, he said, "The Lord is the strength of my life; of whom shall I be afraid?" David knew how to touch God's heart like no other could. Yes, he had troubles, faults, failures, and shortcomings, but he was not too prideful that he would not humble himself before God and reach out to Him for help. We must hold on, persevere, and keep the faith. These hard times won't last always. There is a calmness coming to each of us. We can come out of these troublesome times as "more than conquerors". God is blessing us even though we may not see it. He is keeping us, healing us, and helping us through. God will show up mighty.

James 1:4 Let perseverance finish its work so that you may be mature and complete, not lacking anything.

Romans 8:28 And we know that in all things God works for the good of those who love him, who have been called according to his purpose.

2 Timothy 4:5 But you, keep your head in all situations, endure hardship, do the work of an evangelist, discharge all the duties of your ministry.

POWER OF GOD'S PUNCH

When God's Word is incorporated into your prayers, your prayers become packed with His promises and infused with His power. Jesus said in John 15:7, "If you abide in me, and my words abide in you, ask whatever you wish, and it will be done for you." The heavens and the earth were created by God. He is the power that spoke it into existence. In Genesis 1 He said, "Let there be light!" the light came to the earth, and He created day and night". He is so powerful until darkness had to flee and light appeared. That same power still works. We have to speak His powerful Word and believe. He gives us the power to operate in the power of God. God also parted the Red Sea when Moses trusted God and stretched out his rod. He made the walls of Jericho fall without any tools or machinery. The walls fell because the children of Israel were obedient. At His command, even the moon and the sun must stand still. As we continue this journey of healing and restoration, know that God can do the impossible. He can cause the enemies that you face and see right now to be consumed. Yes, this Pandemic has attacked and caused harm and distress, but God will make everything alright. Whatever your troubles are at this moment, God is about to throw a knockout punch on those issues! Pray fervently, never give up! Help is on the way! God is the same yesterday, today, and forever. He will not fail us. If He helped and rescued the children of Israel from the plagues and evil Pharaoh. Surely, He will deliver us in this chaotic time. He is able to give us Calm in the midst of the Chaos. Just as He brought the children of Israel into the land of promise, He can bring us into a place of peace.

ABOUT THE AUTHOR

Dr. Shelia McGrew is an ordained minister with over 15 years of experience with Ministry, life coaching, elderly and child care, adult care with special needs, child/preteen/teen coaching and more. On May 5, 2018, she obtained her Doctorate of Theology at New Foundation Theological Seminary, Jackson, Mississippi. She hosts her weekly radio and Facebook Live program called PrayerTime w/ Dr. Shelia. Her community achievements include starting the WR McGrew Outreach, Development, and Education Program, a non-profit that encourages social activities and community awareness. Where she serves on the Board of Directors as Vice President. She loves speaking and uplifting others to live a full life on purpose! The reason she became a Life Coach is quite simple. She loves people. In a perfect world, everyone would have positive people in their lives who speak life and gratitude into them. Unfortunately, finding people who are positive, passionate, and genuinely sincere in helping others become the best person they can be, is a daunting task. For years people sought her practical wisdom and advice, listening ear, or just her positive vibe. She is humbled to be that sounding board; that little nudge that could possibly catapult a person into making their dreams reality. She believes that growth will flourish on both sides. Each client that books a session with her will have an opportunity to speak freely without criticism or judgment but with encouragement and support. Join Dr. Shelia and explore the paths of progression towards your hopes and dreams to see what the future will hold.

Website
www.drsheliamcgrew.com

1. Galloway, Nate. (2017). The Shepherd & His Sheep. URL.
2. n.a. (2021). Omnipotent God. URL
3. Spiritual Ray. (2020). *Meaning of 'The Lord is My Shepherd, I Shall not Want' Explained.* Meaning of 'The Lord is My Shepherd, I Shall not Want' Explained. URL.
4. Wellman, Jack. (2021). What Christians Want to Know. 7 Great Bible Verses To Lean On For Tough Decisions. URL.

Made in the USA
Middletown, DE
20 August 2021

46545887R00033